I0808309

FOOD BRANDS WE LOVE

NESTLÉ

By Kaitlyn Duling

Kaleidoscope
Minneapolis, MN

The Quest for Discovery Never Ends

This edition is co-published by agreement between
Kaleidoscope and World Book, Inc.

Kaleidoscope Publishing, Inc.
6012 Blue Circle Drive
Minnetonka, MN 55343 U.S.A.

World Book, Inc.
180 North LaSalle St., Suite 900
Chicago IL 60601 U.S.A.

All rights reserved. No part of this book may be reproduced
in any form without written permission from the publishers.

Kaleidoscope ISBNs
978-1-64519-215-2 (library bound)
978-1-64519-283-1 (ebook)

World Book ISBN
978-0-7166-4193-3 (library bound)

Library of Congress Control Number
2020936232

Text copyright © 2021 by Kaleidoscope Publishing, Inc.
All-Star Sports, Bigfoot Books, and associated logos are
trademarks and/or registered trademarks of Kaleidoscope
Publishing, Inc.

Developed and produced by Focus Strategic Communications Inc.

Printed in the United States of America.

FIND ME IF YOU CAN!

Bigfoot lurks within one of the images in this book. It's up to you to find him!

TABLE OF CONTENTS

Chapter 1
A Big Brand

Leo was on a mission. Nothing could stop him. As the doors slid open, he stepped inside the store. Cold air blasted from the freezers. The air smelled clean. Today was the day that Leo would count every single food company in the grocery store.

Leo's dad often brought him along when he went grocery shopping. They walked up and down the aisles, filling their cart. Leo had always wondered how many different companies were on display at the store. His Dad made him a bet. If he could count them all, he would win $50. Armed with a pen and notebook, Leo started in the frozen food aisle.

Many different products line the shelves at grocery stores.

Many people grocery shop as a family.

He saw Hot Pockets, Lean Cuisine meals, and TombStone pizza. All three went on his list. "Hmm," said Dad, "Those are three types of food, but they are all made by Nestlé. That should count as one company." Leo scratched out his list and wrote "Nestlé."

Nestlé also makes pet food. Purina is their biggest brand. They make dog and cat food under brands such as Purina ONE, Friskies, Beneful, and Fancy Feast.

Next, he wandered into the pet food aisle. Leo wrote down Purina, Friskies, and Beneful. "Hold on," said Dad, "Those are all owned by Nestlé, too." Leo's eyes grew wide. "Is this whole store owned by Nestlé?" Dad just grinned and shook his head.

FUN FACT

Nestlé has a museum in Vevey, Switzerland. It is built on the site of the company's 1866 factory and offices. At the museum, guests can learn about Nestlé chocolate and other foods.

The giant fork is part of a Nestlé exhibit at the Alimentarium in Vevey, Switzerland.

Nestlé Pure Life is a popular water bottle brand.

Leo didn't know it, but Nestlé is the largest food company in the world. Over its 150-year history, the Swiss company has grown. It made over $90 billion in 2019. It **employs** over 300,000 people. Workers produce over 2,000 different products. Nestlé sells baby food, bottled water, coffee, candy, tea, and much more.

FUN FACT

Nescafé, Nestlé's instant coffee brand, is popular around the world. More than 5,500 cups of Nescafé are drunk every second.

Chapter 2

History of Nestlé

How did Nestlé get so big? The story begins over 150 years ago, in 1866. Before there was Nestlé, there were two separate Swiss companies. Two American brothers, Charles and George Page, started a company in Switzerland called the Anglo-Swiss Condensed Milk Company. They produced canned milk.

That same year, a man named Henri Nestlé invented a milk-based baby food. He called his company Farine Lactée Henri Nestlé. "Farine Lactée" means "milk flour." Both companies grew.

In 1877, the Page brothers began producing baby food. The Nestlé company started to sell condensed milk. The two businesses became **rivals**.

Vintage Nestlé chocolates can be seen at the museum in Vevey, Switzerland.

FUN FACT

Switzerland is one of the world's wealthiest countries. It has some of the most famous banks in the world. It is known for its chocolate, cheese, as well as watches and clocks.

In 1905, the two finally decided to **merge**. They formed one company. The focus, at first, was on milk products and chocolate.

As the years passed, Nestlé began to expand its product lines. In 1938, the company began to make coffee. In 1947, it branched into soups. And by the 1950s, it was supplying kitchens with frozen foods. It wasn't until the 1970s that Nestlé began to **diversify**. It bought medical companies. It even bought part of L'Oréal, a makeup brand. Then it

purchased bottled water brands. Pet foods, candies, and cereals came next. Little by little, Nestlé grew into the giant we know today.

WAR AND MILK

During WWI, Nestlé's canned milk became very popular. Why? It lasted a long time. It was also very easy to transport. In 1915, the British army issued Nestlé milk to its soldiers. The Nestlé factories could barely produce enough. By the end of the war, Nestlé had 40 factories. During WWII, Nestlé sold Nescafé to the US military.

NESTLÉ BRAND TIMELINE

1866
Henri Nestlé founds Farine Lactée Henri Nestlé.

1866
George and Charles Page found the Anglo-Swiss Condensed Milk Company.

1867
Nestlé develops its first infant formulas.

1904
Nestlé begins to sell chocolate for the first time.

1905
Henri Nestlé and the Page brothers merge their companies.

1915
The British army issues Nestlé canned milk to soldiers.

1929
Nestlé buys Switzerland's largest chocolate company, Kohler. Chocolate becomes an important part of the company's business.

1938
Nescafé, an instant coffee product, is launched.

1948
Nestea and Nesquik are both introduced.

1866 1867 1904 1905 1915 1929 1938 1948

1973 1976 1985 1988 2001 2007 2010 2016

1973
Seeking to sell more frozen foods, Nestlé buys Stouffer Corporation.

1976
The Nespresso single-serve coffee system is invented.

1985
Nestlé enters the pet food business when it buys Friskies.

1988
Nestlé buys Rowntree's of York, a candy company. The purchase added Aero, Aero Bubbles, KitKat, and Milkybar to Nestlé's candy lineup.

2001
Nestlé purchases popular pet food brand Purina.

2007
Nestlé buys baby food company Gerber, as well as a medical nutrition company called Novartis.

2010
Nestlé gets into the frozen pizza business. It **acquires** DiGiorno, Tombstone, and other top brands from Kraft.

2016
Nestlé celebrates its 150th year.

Chapter 3
Food for Every Age

Sophie grabbed a spoon. The baby was crying. He was hungry. It was Sophie's first time babysitting. She wanted to do everything right. Quickly, Sophie dug through the pantry. She pushed away the cans of soup. She brushed past bags of chips. She couldn't find the baby cereal.

She was getting closer. She picked up a jar of sweet potatoes for babies. But then she saw some pouches of fruit. There was even a jar of kale. Gross. There were yogurt cups and chewy biscuits. This baby had more options than the school cafeteria. Sophie frowned as she picked up a box of baby cereal. This was the one. Sophie hoped he would like it.

Most pantries are filled with Nestlé products.

The Gerber baby is iconic.

Sophie looked closely at every jar, pouch, and box. Each one had the Gerber or Nestlé **logo** on it. That made sense. Gerber has been in the baby food business since 1927. Back then, Daniel and

In 1974, Gerber tried to sell baby food...for adults. Its "Singles by Gerber" meals were packaged in glass jars. Flavors like "beef burgundy" were meant to be eaten with a spoon. Gerber hoped college students and young people would gobble up the meals. But the packaging—and the idea—did not find fans. Many consider it to be one of the biggest food fails of all time.

Dorothy Gerber sold the infant food from their family canning factory in Michigan. It was a hit. Nestlé bought the company in 2007.

Gerber has many different kinds of food for babies and toddlers.

Gerber packages are a good way for babies to get their fruits and veggies.

The purchase of Gerber made sense. Infant cereal was one of the first products sold by Henri Nestlé in the 1860s. There is a story that the early cereal saved the life of a baby boy named Wanner. In the 21st century, infant formulas and foods are still a big part of the Nestlé business.

THE FACE OF GERBER

In 1928, Gerber held a contest. They wanted to find a face to put on their baby food labels. Artist Dorothy Hope Smith drew a simple picture. It became the face of the brand. For decades, people wondered who the "real" Gerber baby was. They wondered if it was a boy or a girl. After 40 years, the truth was revealed. Hope had used her neighbor, Ann Turner Cook, as the model.

Chapter 4
Candy Confusion

Miles broke off a piece of his KitKat bar. The “snap” made him smile. He took a bite. It was sweet. Miles glanced down at the wrapper. Something wasn’t right. KitKat was made by Hershey. But this wrapper had the Nestlé logo on it.

Miles was confused. But there's a simple way to unwrap the mystery. You just have to know the history. The first KitKat was launched in England in 1935. Back then, KitKats were made by Rowntree's of York. At first, it was called Rowntree's Chocolate Crisp. Nestlé acquired Rowntree's in 1988.

FUN FACT

KitKats were originally made to fit inside a packed lunch. That's where they get their square shape. In England, fans enjoyed eating the candy during their tea break. That's where the idea of the KitKat "break" was born.

Nestlé makes KitKats in more than 80 countries. The only difference? In the US, the KitKat brand is **licensed** to Reese's. Reese's is owned by Hershey. That's just a complicated way of saying that Hershey has the right to produce KitKats in the US, but Nestlé does not.

When Miles unwrapped his Nestlé KitKat, he was eating a candy bar made outside the US. Perhaps he was eating a Coconut KitKat from Prague. Or a Caramel KitKat from Hong Kong. Nestlé sells dozens of unique KitKat flavors around the world.

There are many different KitKat flavors around the world.

FUN FACT

In 2019, KitKat opened a store in Toronto, Canada. It is called the KitKat Chocolatory. At the store, customers can create their own KitKat flavors. There are over 2,000 flavor combinations available. Options include potato chips, rose petals, and gummy bears.

LUCKY KITKAT

In Japan, KitKats are often seen as a sign of good luck. They are very popular, and they come in wild flavors. Blueberry cheesecake, apple, and green tea are just a few of the options. Would you eat a hot chili KitKat? What about baked potato? There's even a "cough drop" flavor.

NESTLÉ

TOP BRANDS

1. Gerber (Baby Foood)

2. S. Pellegrino (Water)

3. Cheerios (Cereal)

4. KitKat (Chocolate)

5. Nespresso (Coffee)

6. Stouffer's (Gourmet Food)

7. Carnation (Dairy)

8. Nestea (Drinks)

BEYOND THE BOOK

After reading the book, it's time to think about what you learned. Try the following exercises to jumpstart your ideas.

THINK

THAT'S NEWS TO ME. Nestlé is often in the news. Consider how you learn about foods and brands. What information can be found in news articles? What about news programs on TV? Where can you go to find news you can trust?

CREATE

PRIMARY SOURCES. Primary sources provide firsthand accounts of an event. Interviews, videos, and photographs are all examples of primary sources. Create a list of the kinds of primary sources you might be able to find about Nestlé.

SHARE

WHAT'S YOUR OPINION? The text states that Nestlé is a giant company. Do you agree with that statement? Provide evidence from the text to support your opinion. Share your position and evidence with a friend. Does your friend find the argument convincing?

GROW

DRAWING CONNECTIONS. Create a diagram that shows and explains connections between Nestlé and its many brands. How does learning about the history help you better understand Nestlé?